Black Masters:
A Side-light on Slavery

Calvin Dill Wilson
(1857–1946)

Originally published
1904

BLACK MASTERS

THE most singular and dramatic aspect of slavery in the United States was the occasional ownership of bondsmen by free blacks. Historically, the facts are obscure, little known and difficult to trace; this phase is overlooked by historians, so far as I am aware, and is lost from the memories of most people of this generation; I have asked dozens of Southern people, of advanced years, about negroes owning slaves, and have been told that they "never heard of such a thing." Psychologically, after all we have read and heard of the pathos and tragedy of negro slavery, it is of strange interest and unaccountable inconsistency that the negroes themselves should at times have had no apparent compunction in regard to buying their fellows at the block, continuing them in enforced and unremunerated toil, and at times treating them with cruelty and reducing them to the depths of humiliation and degradation. The mere lust of gain by the toil of others could not altogether account for this wrench of nature, since slave labor could be hired as well as bought, and hired workers would have served the ends of greed as well or better. It would commonly have been cheaper for a free black to hire the slaves of others than to risk his money in their ownership, and to provide lodgings, clothes and food for them. In many cases the free blacks did pursue this course. But there was a deeper passion than love of gain in this unnatural arrangement, and this was ambition; it was the cold and selfish desire to attain a real or an apparent superiority over other blacks; it was ambition to rise into the class of masters, and to stand, so far as possible, on the same level as white men.

But there were those who had far different motives. Free colored men sometimes owned their wives and children; and free colored women owned their families, and continued this ownership for reasons that were creditable to them. By this legal possession they kept the members of their families safe from the operation of local laws that were invidious to free blacks. Some of the States had laws that bore hard on free blacks; for certain periods there were laws that compelled a manumitted slave to leave his State; thus a negro who freed his family might have decreed their separation from himself. There were, also, free blacks who purchased others for the purpose of manumitting them; but this class is not of importance to us in discussing the actual ownership of slaves by free blacks.

It may be of interest to the reader to indicate something of the obscurity of this subject by a few statements. I know of no history of the United States, or history of slavery or history of a slave State that even hints at it, with the exception of one book which will presently be mentioned. My researches, while an effort has been made to be thorough, may have overlooked books that touch upon it. But the Librarian of Congress directed me to one volume only, and that but barely glances at the subject. From other librarians I have been able to get no assistance, save in another instance in which I was directed to the volume spoken of above. Mr. Booker T. Washington wrote: "My own personal recollections bring no cases to mind of free black men owning slaves, nor am I able to refer you to any books making reference to this phase of slavery, in case it did exist." General Warren Keifer, who is particularly well versed in American history, wrote: "I have no data to which I could refer you on the subject of the ownership of negro slaves by free negroes." Dr. George Archer, one of the best local historians in Maryland, could only say that he could not give me the desired information, though he recalled a single item from the local records of Harford County, Maryland, in which a free negro had owned and had freed one or more slaves, but after search he was unable to find this item. He gave, however, instances in which free negroes bought their wives and children from their masters and emancipated them; all so emancipated were, by an Act of Assembly in 1831, required to be sent out of the State, the Orphan's Court being empowered to allow them to remain if so minded. The same gentleman later wrote that he had made inquiries at the county seat, had put the question to all the prominent lawyers of the bar who often had reason to search the records on all manner of subjects; but none of them had ever seen or heard of a case of the kind. He next inquired of the County Clerk and the Register of Wills, who have held their respective positions for many years, and their answers were identical with those of the legal fraternity. He then got their directions as to where in the records he would be most likely to find such items, if existing, and made researches accordingly; but not a trace could he find. He then questioned several persons noted for their fondness for inquiries in local history; but the result was the same. He then searched the histories of Maryland, from Bozman to Scharf, but with like result. The Virginia State Librarian wrote that he was unable to obtain any information concerning slaves held by free blacks, though he believed such ownership had been practised in Virginia; but he stated that it was a very common thing in Louisiana. A prominent colored man of Mound Bayou, Mississippi, to whom I had been referred by Booker Washington, Isaiah T. Montgomery, stated: "I do not remember that I ever saw any free colored people prior to Emancipation, and believe there were few, if any, instances where they owned slaves in this State. I have, however, heard that this condition prevailed in some of the sugar districts of Louisiana, and your communication has been referred to a competent friend in that State." He wrote me again stating that he had interviewed an aged colored man, whom he called "Father Johnson," who was "one of our most highly respected ante-bellum citizens," and belonged to "what was known as the favored class." This aged man said, in regard to free colored people residing in the South prior to the war: "There was very little pleasure in their existence. Every year they were compelled to have fresh papers filed by some white guardian. They were not allowed to be visited by slaves or to have companionship with them. When attending church, walking the roads, in fact in all places, they were compelled to keep apart from slaves."

The Clerk of Talbot County, Maryland, wrote that "no such condition existed in this county, and there are no records of such a condition"; the like officer of Queen Anne County made a similar reply. As the court-house of Frederick County was burned a number of years ago, there is no means of ascertaining conditions there; Worcester County has no such records. The Clerk of Princess Anne Court-house wrote that "such a thing as a negro owning another of his race was not known in this county." The Rev. Dr. A.M. Green, of the General Conference of the A.M.E. Church, wrote from New Orleans:

"There is any quantity of traditionary information, but you know that it is not worth much in a search after truth. I have heard a great deal along the line of this inquiry, but very little that could be vouched for. Among the official Board and Quarterly Conference proceedings of St. James's Chapel, A.M.E., I have read of three cases being tried for owning slaves; in each of these cases it was made apparent to the satisfaction of the church that the owners of slaves thus charged had purchased them for the sole purpose of emancipating them. These cases occurred between 1849 and 1856; when, where or how the emancipation took place, if ever, does not appear among the records of St. James's. These trials were for violation of the Discipline and Rules of our church. I suppose there are but few persons now living who know anything of the events of that period in our church. There are many things along this line of great interest to me, and to others if they could be so brought out as to attract the attention of the New Negro as well as the New White youth of our country North and South."

This letter gives us the additional information that the owning of slaves by free negroes was contrary to the Discipline of the A.M.E. Church; by inference, the practice could not have been uncommon, or there would have been no reason for ecclesiastical rulings. Dr. Hodges, of the Cincinnati Public Library, informed me that some years ago there was pointed out to him in Statesburg, South Carolina, a house, with iron-barred windows, in which he was told a negro blacksmith, who had been noted for cruelty to his slaves, had been used to confine his blacks. Mr. Alexander Hill, one of the best-informed men on books in Cincinnati, was unable to give any clue to information upon this matter, except to direct me to correspond with the editor of "The

Antiquary," at Norfolk, Virginia. On correspondence with Mr. Edward W. James, at the Virginia Club, Norfolk, I learned that "The Antiquary" contains a few references to negroes owning slaves.

Mr. Florien Giaugus, of Glendale, Ohio, suggested that I write to Mr. Charles W. Elam, a prominent lawyer at Mansfield, Louisiana, who was able to say only, "I have been unable to find any witnesses in this parish of the ownership of negroes by free blacks"; but he gave me references to gentlemen who might afford me information. The Hon. B.F. Jonas, of New Orleans, replied:

"A great many slaves were owned by free blacks before the war, not only in this State, but throughout the South. In this State, there were quite a large number of colored slave-owners, most of whom were of the class known as 'quadroons,' but some of them were mulattoes and full-blood negroes, who, as a rule, inherited property and afterward added to it, probably by purchase. Free colored people had a right to the ownership and possession of slave property, as well as movable property and other real estate,—slave property having been considered real estate under our laws at that period. I have never heard of a case where a free black owner of slaves voluntarily manumitted his slaves. On the contrary, they were as a rule considered hard task masters, who got out of their slave property all that they could. I suppose that proof of this and the names of slave-owners could be obtained from an examination of the assessment rolls of the City of New Orleans and the parishes, previous to the war; but this is so long ago that the information could probably not be obtained without a great deal of labor and investigation."

The Hon. Phanor Breazeale, of Natchitoches, Louisiana, to whom Mr. Elam also referred me, wrote:

"This, Natchitoches, my own town, is the oldest town of the Louisians. Purchase, and the legal records date back to 1708. The Parish, synonymous with County, is one of the largest in territory and population in the State, and of recent years has been known as a black county, that is to say, the negro population was a little in excess of the white population. Assuming that the records of the Parish are a fair criterion by which to judge the other old parishes of the State, it was not an uncommon feature of slavery to find that free blacks owned slaves; but, on the contrary, there were, prior to the war, quite a number of 'free colored people,' as they were called, who were owners of slaves; some of these free colored people in this Parish were quite wealthy. I have in mind a lawsuit I brought a few years ago for the ownership of a piece of land in this Parish; and, in the course of litigation, I traced back the title about eighty years, and found that there was a French nobleman settled here who reared a family of negroes, living in concubinage with a 'free colored woman'; they had several children; of course he never married the woman and his children were illegitimate, but free as being the issue of a white man and free colored woman. He left a will giving his property one-half to the mother of his children and the remainder in equal portions to the children. The inventory in this succession was appraised at some one hundred and three thousand dollars, including lands and slaves. This will was contested by a brother who lived in France, and resulted in a compromise whereby the children were given a large plantation with ten slaves, the mother getting the usufruct of this property. This is an instance of the conditions existing at that time. The records here disclose sales to, and from, free colored people of slaves. I do not recall any instance, in examining the records, of having found a case where a free black owner voluntarily manumitted his slaves. It is very probable that a careful investigation of the records would disclose instances where some particular slave was manumitted by his free black owner from motives of attachment, by reason of loyal and faithful service to the owner; but I do not believe the records will disclose any case of manumission of all the slaves owned by free black persons. This latter, as you know, has very frequently been done by white owners; for instance, my great-grandfather, a lawyer of prominence, owned many slaves both in Mississippi and in Louisiana, and by will manumitted all his slaves and provided for their transportation to Africa. As a matter of interest in studying this phase of slavery, I have found by inquiry from old people that free black owners were as a usual thing much more severe on their slaves than the white owners. Personally, I know nothing of these facts, as I was born too late; yet I feel that the above criticism is correct, not only because it can be reconciled with phases of human nature, but because of the fact that now in this Parish the colony of 'free colored people' have preserved in the forty years since the war absolutely intact their status, and have positively refused to come in contact with the freed slaves, either socially or otherwise. These 'free colored people' were a distinct type, as you no doubt know; they were either quadroons or octoroons, and not manumitted slaves. If a negro ever became owner of slaves after his manumission, it is not known, so far as the records show or I have been able to learn by inquiry."

That the free negroes had not always conscience or sentiment against slavery is indicated by the fact that James Clark, a free negro, enlisted in Company K, Twenty-eighth

BLACK MASTERS

Georgia Regiment (Captain Wilcox), as a fifer, and went through the Civil War; he is now 104 years old, and has applied for a pension from the State of Georgia for service in the Confederate army. We may presume that he knew that the success of his cause would, in all probability, have continued slavery. Mr. E.W. James comments thus on "Betsy Fuller, Free Black, and her husband":

"The wife owned the husband. It was not an uncommon thing in the Southern States for enterprising negro women to own their husbands. At the outbreak of the War of Secession, an industrious negress, a huckstress in the Norfolk market, owned her husband. He was an ardent secessionist, and was in full sympathy with the firing on and the fall of Fort Sumter. After Norfolk was evacuated and was occupied by the Federal forces, he was loud in his expression of Southern views, and was at one time in the chain gang, with an iron ball attached to one of his feet, because of expression of opinions obnoxious to the military. No slavetrader was ever more fully convinced that the negroes were made for slavery."

BLACK MASTERS

Our present views of slavery had not universally penetrated the minds of the colored people themselves in ante-bellum days! Father Johnson, already referred to, wrote:

"A white man named Fitzgerald, a planter, owned a plantation and slaves in the vicinity of Natchez, Adams County, Mississippi, and he had as a wife a very dark colored woman; they had two sons, George and James Fitzgerald. At the death of the father, the plantation and slaves were inherited by the children under a will. The slaves and plantation were held by the heirs until freed by the War. Both of the Fitzgerald boys selected slave women, belonging to a Colonel Wood, as wives, and sought to purchase them. Colonel Wood declined to sell, but consented to what was known as 'blanket marriages.' The younger son, James, afterward gave up his wife, although several children had been born to them, and finally left the country, declaring that he did not want a slave woman for a wife. The elder brother, George, remained and continued to consort with his slave wife, up to his death after the War. He grieved himself to death over the results of the War, by which he lost his slaves. Colonel Wood filed papers regularly every year as George Fitzgerald's guardian, according to the law which required that free negroes should annually file papers proving their right to freedom. The mother of these men, old Mrs. Fitzgerald, was somewhat careful of her slaves; when it rained, she would have them come in from the garden."

Mr. D.C. Scarborough, of Natchitoches, Louisiana, wrote:

"There are many data to be had by examining the old records of this Parish on the subject of the purchase, ownership and sale of slaves by free blacks. The truth of the matter is that free blacks owned, bought and sold slaves as did the whites. The succession of C.N. Roques in this Parish is a case in which a free black owned some hundred or so slaves, all of whom were freed by the Proclamation of Emancipation. We do not recollect any special legislation authorizing the ownership of negroes by free blacks.

BLACK MASTERS

When a slave became free he bought and sold fully under the law, just as any other citizen did; there was no longer any distinction. In many of the old deeds it is recited that A.B., 'being a free person of color,' etc. History will show that the free blacks who owned slaves rarely if ever emancipated them. Slaves who were emancipated were, as a rule, emancipated by white owners; and this emancipation by white owners is the manner in which free blacks came into existence. There was a very large number of these in this Parish, some of the richest people in the Parish being free persons of color. On tracing back the history of these families, it is generally found that they were emancipated by former white owners.

There are four or five such families that married and intermarried until they were all related. In some instances, there were to be found as many as one hundred and fifty voters in one ward of these free persons of color; their descendants live here yet. As a rule, these families took the name of their former master who freed them. A large per cent. of those in this parish are named Metoyer, one of the old rich Metoyers having freed some of his slaves. The same is true of the Dupré family and of the Rachal family; there being as many free colored Rachals as there were White at the close of the war. This general outline can be very generally verified by copies of old records here.

We are to remember, in connection with the conditions in Louisiana, that a general trait of French and Spanish colonists in all countries has been that they have commonly recognized and provided for the wives taken from among native women, negro, Indian, or any other nationality, and that they have acknowledged and provided for their children; while the AngloSaxon, as a rule, leaves these women and children to shift for themselves.

But in Maryland still other phases of this matter are to be studied. In Maryland, pure blacks who had themselves been slaves and had been manumitted were frequently slave owners. In that State, also, we are able to find instances of a kind asserted by some of our Louisiana correspondents to have been unknown in their own, of voluntary manumissions by these black masters of their slaves; and not only the emancipation of their slave wives and children, but of all those whom they held in bondage, thus indicating a change of heart in the matter. For this latter condition there were several contributing causes; one of these was that in Maryland, in the latter part of the eighteenth century, Emancipation Societies were active, manumission by white owners was common, and the influence of this conduct spread to the free colored people who held other colored people in bondage.

It will be of interest to consider briefly some of the general conditions of the free negro and of the emancipation spirit in Maryland. On this subject, much valuable information can be gotten from "The Negro in Maryland, A Study of Slavery," by Jeffrey R. Brackett, the volume indicated to me by the Librarian of Congress as the only book he knew which bore upon my immediate inquiry about free negroes who owned slaves and manumitted them; upon this particular point, however, the volume contains very little. About the year 1785, several Abolition Societies arose in Maryland and began uninterrupted work toward emancipation. Petitions were presented by them to the Legislature tending toward gradual abolition. In 1752, manumission in any way, during the last illness of the master, had been forbidden; but these Societies induced the Legislature to remove all restrictions from the voluntary emancipation of slaves. During the last decade of the eighteenth century there was a large increase in the number of slaves manumitted.

Many of these manumissions were accompanied by grants of land from the masters. In 1747, "a citizen of Queen Anne County freed several slaves by his will, and also gave to them and their heirs a tract of land. A certain citizen by will freed nineteen slaves and gave them a great part of his real and personal estate; a niece of the testator attempted to break the will, but after several years of contest the will was established. A law was enacted that all slaves unable to support themselves should be supported by their masters, "in fitting food and clothing," and kept from begging. This legislation was caused by the fact that some masters had used their slaves as long as they were profitable and had then turned them adrift to burden the community. Under the new ruling, slaves to be manumitted must be sound in mind and body, capable of labor and not over fifty years of age. It was enacted that all manumissions must be in writing, under hand and seal of two witnesses; the papers to be acknowledged and endorsed by a justice, and then recorded within six months in the clerk's office of the county. The cost for recording a deed of manumission was the ordinary trivial fee for record; and a certified copy of a deed was deemed good evidence of freedom.

The number of free colored persons in Maryland was small, and there was little mention of them until the close of the eighteenth century. Griffith's "Annals of Baltimore" states that the population of Baltimore County, including the later

Harford County, in 1752 included one hundred and sixteen mulatto slaves, one hundred and ninety-six free mulattoes, four thousand and twenty-seven negro slaves and eight free negroes. "The distinction between negroes and mulattoes is interesting," says Mr. Brackett; and this distinction is to be kept in mind in noting the manumissions in Maryland. When a "free negro" manumits, it means that this is done by a negro, not by a mulatto. The census of 1790 gives about eight thousand free colored persons in the State; some of these, or their ancestors, had come as free men, most had been manumitted. By the Convention of 1776, the right of suffrage was given to all freemen who held a certain amount of property; and it is certain that some free negroes voted in the early years of the State. In 1782, the Assembly of Virginia passed an Act permitting the manumission of slaves; Judge Tucker of Virginia estimated that, from 1782 to 1791, ten thousand slaves were liberated in Virginia by their masters.

BLACK MASTERS

There were many free negroes in Maryland who owned small houses and pieces of land.

"The acts of incorporation of some savings-banks limited depositors to white persons; others could receive from any persons. In Annapolis, for instance, several free blacks were depositors, and one at least owned shares of the bank stock.

"From the earliest history of Maryland, free negroes have been allowed to sue in the courts, as well as to hold both real and personal property. The education of free negroes and of slaves was not forbidden by law in Maryland; but the black was indebted for what he got to the interest of individuals or of such societies as the Society of Friends."

Mr. Brackett says:

"Free negroes not infrequently owned as slaves their wives and children, whom they feared, perhaps, to manumit, lest the right to residence be questioned. It would seem also that other free negroes owned and hired slaves, as did their white neighbors.

We hear of one free black, of Dorchester County, receiving payment for a slave whom he had bought for a term of years, and who was sold out of the State for crime by the court. In 1827 a member for the same county had introduced a bill to forbid anyone who owned slaves for life, or for a term of years, from hiring such to a free negro there. Kent and Somerset were added to Dorchester and, later, Worcester and Anne Arundel were added and Kent struck out; and the Committee on Grievances, ordered to inquire into the expediency of preventing free blacks from purchasing slaves under any circumstances, reported that any legislation on the subject was inexpedient."

Mr. Brackett wrote during a visit to England:

"I regret that I am unable to help you, as my book was written a good while ago, and my odd notes of information not given in the book have not been kept. The position of free negroes in Maryland in the last years of the eighteenth century was interesting; a few of them voted, and were full-fledged citizens."

An aged man, William W. Davis, eighty-eight years of age, who lives at Cambridge, Maryland, wrote concerning one Draper Thompson, free negro, who in 1824 bought and sold a negro man at public auction out of an estate for three hundred dollars. The record of this purchase is in the Dorchester County records (E. R., No. 9, folios 179 and 180). Mr. Davis says he knew Thompson well in his own boyhood, that at one time he lived on a large farm, the Cremona Tract; he did not allow his slaves to associate with his own family, but made them eat and sleep in a separate house; if a slave had occasion to enter his dwelling, he had to doff his hat and carry it under his arm while doing so. He sent his sons to Baltimore for an education. Mr. Davis adds: "Make a slave an overseer over his fellow slaves, as sometimes happened, and he would be three times as tyrannical as a white man."

Philip Roberts, a respectable colored man of Glendale, Ohio, who was a slave in Kentucky, told me that he knew "Old Free Isaac," in Trimble County, Kentucky, who owned several negroes; he said this same negro sold his own son and daughter South, one for $1,000, the other for $1,200.

Mr. Stevenson Archer, of Mississippi, states that he knew a pure-blooded negro, born free, by name Nori (a corruption of Le Noir), who had before the Civil War a large plantation in Mississippi, and owned about one hundred negroes. He was exacting, but not cruel, and he took excellent care of his slaves.

Mr. Charles Michael, of Harford County, Maryland, remembers the case of a negro who sold his children in order to purchase his wife. There were many instances in which negroes, who had purchased their own freedom and secured the ownership of their families, sold their children for life or for a term of years.

We give below citations from Maryland county records in which free negroes manumitted their slaves. The first instances are those of the freeing of wives and children:

"Know all men, by these presents, that I, Robert, lately a slave to Archibald Pattison, deceased, and sold by Peter Gordon, Administrator of said Archibald Pattison, to John Griffith, by whom I was manumitted, according to law, do hereby, in consideration of the natural affection I bear to Rachel, whom I have taken as my wife, and whom I purchased of John Le Compte, deceased, manumit, enfranchise and set at liberty the said Rachel from me, my heirs, Exor's &. Admrs, from the date of these presents, in as perfect a manner as if she had been born so.'" (March 9th, 1796. Record H. D., No. 9, fol. 1653, Dorchester Co.)

"Manumission by Cato, negro, of Dorchester County, Maryland—

"'Being possessed of a wife and children who are by law my slaves, and being desirous to set them free, etc., wife Lucy, children, Leah, Milly, Mary, Horatio, Ephraim and Abraham.'" (April 30th, 1798. Record H. D., No. 12, fol. 633, Dorchester 00.)

"Manumission by Adam, negro, of Dorchester County, State of Maryland, of negro Phillis—'Having purchased my wife Phillis, and being desirous to secure her her liberty, etc., do therefore set free the said Phillis immediately.'" (Aug. 17th, 1797. Record H. D., No. 12, fol. 255, Don-heater (70.)

"Manumission by Oliver Cromwell, negro, of Dorchester County, State of Maryland, to Shadrach Cromwell—'Do release from slavery, etc., my son Shadrach Cromwell, acknowledging the said negro slave discharged, etc.'" (Feb. 5th, 1818. Record E. R., No. 15, folio 16.)

"Manumission by John Chapman, negro, of Dorchester County, State of Maryland, of Mary Chapman, negro—'Being 37 years of age and able to work and gain a sufficient livelihood, etc., do set free, etc.'" (March 14th, 1818. Record E. R., No. 5, folio 40.)

The further citations are those of cases in which there was manumission by free negroes of slaves not related to them:

"Manumission by Henry Hughes, negro, of Dorchester County, State of Maryland, of negro, Ruth—'Being possessed of a negro woman—Ruth, and desirous to give her her legal manumission, etc.'" (Dec. 14th, 1816. Record E. R., No. 4, folio 297.)

"Manumission by John Driver, negro, of Dorchester County, State of Maryland, to sundry negroes—'Do set free and hereby release from slavery, 6 in number.'" (May 28th, 1825. Record E. R., No. 9, folio 614.)

The three records that follow form a connected story; first the negro is himself set free by his white master:

"Deed of manumission from William Meeds Satterfield, of Caroline County, to 'my negro man, Jem,' dated 10 June, 1790; acknowledged before Dr. Zabdiel Potter, of the commission of the peace for Caroline County, 10 June 1790; recorded in Liber W. R., No. 0., fol. 118, on the 17th of June, A.D. 1790, by William Richardson, Clerk.

"'State of Maryland, Caroline County, to wit:

"'Whereas, a certain Black man, by the name of James Satterfield, heretofore, to wit: on the 10th day of June, 1790, was manumitted by a certain William Meeds Satterfield, to be free from the date thereof; and whereas the said Black man, James Satterfield, hath made application to me for a certificate of his freedom, agreeable to an Act of Assembly: Upon the oath of Elijah Satterfield that the said Black man, called James Satterfield, is the identical person who was manumitted as aforesaid, I do hereby certify that the said Black man, called James Satterfield, is five feet three inches high, has small scar on his left hand made by the bite of a hog, and from the age expressed in the aforesaid manumission is about fifty-five years of age, was raised in Queen Anne County, in Tulley's Neck, and was removed to this county about the age of twenty-four years, and no other notable marks that I can discover (sic). In testimony whereof I have set my hand and affixed the public seal of my office this tenth day of May, in the year of Our Lord 1808. Tho: Richardson, Clk. Caroline Co.: Ct.'" (Recorded in Liber T. R., Certificates of Freedom, fol. 23.)

Now James has taken to slave-holding himself, but resolves to provide for the freedom of his slaves at his death:

"Caroline County, to wit:

"Be it remembered, That on the 19th day of October, in the year of our Lord 1802, came James Satterfield, free negro, and brought a manumission, with one endorsement thereon, and prayed to have the same enrolled amongst the Records of Caroline County; and on the same 19th day of Oct., in the year 1802, afsd., the same manumission and endorsement were enrolled as follows, to wit:

"'I, James Satterfield, free negro, of Caroline County and State of Maryland, do hereby set free from bondage, after my decease, one negro girl named Rachel, and one by the name of Hannah, which two girls I purchased of Elijah Satterfield, executor or administrator of William Fountain, late of the county afsd., deceased, and do for myself, my heirs, executors and administrators, or assigns, release unto the afsd. Rachel and Hannah, after my decease, all my right, and all my claim whatsoever, to be absolutely free from me or from my heirs, executors, administrators or assigns, or from any other person or persons whatsoever, thereby claiming any right or title whatsoever by, from or under me, or them.

"'In witness hereof, I have hereunto set my hand and seal, this 19th day of the tenth month, 1802.

"'James Satterfield X his mark. (Seal.)'

"Signed sealed and delivered in the presence of James Dixon, Seth Hill Evitts.

"Recorded in Liber T.R., No. H., folio 228, a Land Record for Caroline County, Md. Tho: Richardson, Clerk."

But, some years later, James decides to give these girls their freedom before his death. So we read:

"Deed of manumission by James Satterfield, negro, dated the 29th day of October, 1823, 'I, James Satterfield, negro, of

Caroline County in the State of Maryland, for divers good causes and considerations me thereunto moving, do hereby declare free, manumit and enfranchise the negroes following, to wit: Hannah, about thirty-four years of age, on the first day of May last past; Kitty, about fifteen years of age, the second day of April last past; Rachel, about twelve years of age the fifteenth day of January last past; James, about nine years of age the seventh day of January last past; and Matthew, about five years of age the fifth day of May last past. Which said last-mentioned four negroes, viz.: Kitty, Rachel, James and Matthew, are the children of Hannah, also above mentioned. Rachel, about thirty-two years of age the first day of May last past, and her child, a negro boy called James, about six years of age in September last.'

"Recorded in Liber J. R., No. 0., fol. 208, on the 29th day of October, 1823. Joseph Richardson, Clerk."

The following is the will of a free negro, named Ricksum Webb. It appears from memories of him that still survive that he was a rather superior man. He left several hundreds of acres of land, a large personal estate, and his descendants are now among the representative negroes in Caroline County. The name of Webb is a synonym for industry, thrift and intelligence in that county and is borne by many negroes. A like reputation is sustained by the Friends, mainly descended from Gabriel Friend, who was freed in the thirties by a white master. Ricksum Webb's son, James, owned one or more slaves up to the time of the Emancipation.

"Last will and Testament of Ricksum Webb, (negro), recorded in Will Record W. A. F., No. A., fol. 357, et sq. Directs that my servant Jerry shall serve my son James for the period of ten years after death of testator, and then to be free; to be given $50 a year during this service, and suitable clothing. Should Jerry abscond from service and be taken, to be sold for life to the highest bidder. In lieu of this service, to be sold to a resident of Maryland for not less than $400 for a period of ten years and then to be free.

BLACK MASTERS

Said Jerry to have choice of purchasers. Servant Luke willed to son-in-law, Eben Hughes. Servant Asbury to be free at age of 35 years. Girl servant Ann to be free at age of 25. James Turner, of Queen Anne's, executor. Will dated 10 May, 1845. Proven, 27th March, 1846, before William A. Ford, Register of Wills for Caroline County."

Thus these dark faces look out upon us from the past, and the records and names from musty folios in old Maryland courthouses tell of a singular aspect of slavery.

CALVIN DILL WILSON.

BLACK MASTERS

www.ingramcontent.com/pod-product-compliance
Lightning Source LLC
Chambersburg PA
CBHW020332290526
45785CB00007B/3024